ORGANIZING INFORMATION

Lack of organization can make you feel overwhelmed by all the things you have to do.

THE LEARNING-A-LIVING LIBRARY

High Performance Through
ORGANIZING
INFORMATION

Carolyn Simpson

THE ROSEN PUBLISHING GROUP, INC.
NEW YORK

Published in 1996 by The Rosen Publishing Group, Inc.
29 East 21st Street, New York, NY 10010

Copyright 1996 by The Rosen Publishing Group, Inc.

First Edition

Printed in the United States of America

Library of Congress Cataloging-in-Publication Data

Simpson, Carolyn.
    Organizing information / Carolyn Simpson.
      p. cm. — (The learning-a-living library)
    Includes bibliographical references and index.
    Summary: Provides an overview of organizing skills for use at
home, at school, and in a future career.
    ISBN 0-8239-2207-3
    1. Time management—Juvenile literature. 2. Records—Management—
Juvenile literature. 3. Life skills—Juvenile literature.
[1. Time management. 2. Life skills.] I. Title. II. Series.
HD69.T54S58 1996
640'.43—dc20   95-39724
                                                CIP
                                                 AC

Contents

	Introduction	7
1)	Finding Information in School	11
2)	Organizing Information in School	16
3)	Organizing Your Life	22
4)	Organizing Your Work Environment	30
5)	Keeping on Top of Jobs	37
6)	Getting the Job	43
7)	Organizing for Performance	49
	Glossary	61
	For Further Reading	62
	Index	63

Even a simple organizer like a bulletin board can become confusing if it is overloaded with information.

Introduction

MICHELLE WAS TOO TIRED TO STUDY ANY LONGER, so she wrote herself a note: "Finish math!" She placed it on her desk on top of her math book so she'd see it first thing in the morning.

The next morning Michelle overslept. She grabbed a quick breakfast and hopped in the shower, forgetting all about her math homework. When she put her books into her backpack, she knocked the note onto the floor. She never even saw it.

As she opened her room door, she glanced at several notes taped to the frame: "Call Marsha about game Saturday!" "Bring money for pictures Wednesday!" "French test Monday!"

I've got to put these notes in order, she thought. There are too many to remember.

As she raced for the bus, her mother called, "Would you start dinner for me tonight, Michelle? I'll be working late."

"Just leave me a note," Michelle called back. "Put it where I'll see it."

Some people like Michelle make a good attempt at organizing their lives, but they go about it the wrong way. They write notes to remind themselves of things to do and places to be. But the problem is that after a while their notes get buried under more notes, and nothing gets done.

When these people write reports, they run into the same problem. The don't know how to organize the material, so they start writing about one thing and end up writing about something else. Then they remember a point they should have made in the beginning and stick it in at the end. It's up to the teacher to make sense of the report.

Some people think they'll learn how to be organized when they're older. They don't realize that we create habits when we're young, and habits are hard to break. In the high performance workplace, employers are looking for people who are good organizers. People who can organize the information around them are better focused and get things done. They know how to keep track of meetings and deadlines. They know how to find information and store it until needed. They know how to put together reports, memos, and letters. They can think clearly and get their points across to others.

Information skills are needed for all kinds of jobs. Bookkeepers and managers deal with figures and reports. Secretaries, receptionists, and clerks deal with memos, reports, letters, and files. Teachers need to keep track of grades. Bill collectors need to keep track of accounts, and politicians need to stay on top of how people are voting. In fact, every job requires dealing with some amount of information.

Getting a job and keeping it is a lot harder these days. After all, more people are competing for the same jobs. When an employer sees a desk buried under files and notes, what do you think she's thinking? Probably she's thinking that the employee can't stay on top of his workload. Maybe she thinks the rest of his life is out of control, too.

Clearly, being organized is important.

Your school library is full of useful information.

Finding Information in School

HENRY AND MARK WENT TO THE LIBRARY. BOTH were doing reports on natural disasters in American history. Henry remembered learning the Dewey Decimal System in English class, so he knew that all the nonfiction books in the library were organized according to subject. All he had to do was figure out what subject would fit "natural disaster." Then he could look up the category and see what its number was.

He couldn't decide whether it would fit under "Science" or "History," so he thought he'd try both. He spent the next twenty minutes walking up and down the aisles looking for a suitable book.

Meanwhile, Mark took a different approach. He sat down at the library computer and looked up "natural disasters" in the subject index. The computer suggested that he look up specific subjects, such as tornadoes, hurricanes, fires, and floods. As he narrowed down his choices, he found the exact books he wanted and their reference numbers. He didn't have to walk the aisles to find them; he went to the shelves with the corresponding Dewey Decimal numbers.

Both guys found the information they wanted. Henry found his books almost by accident and never knew that better books might already be checked out. If they weren't there on the shelf, he didn't know they existed. Mark already knew what books he'd have to request from other libraries even before he approached the shelves.

Your school or public library is an example of a place where a great deal of information must be organized so that it is easy to use. If all the books in the library were simply sitting in one big pile, you'd probably never find what you wanted when you went to find a novel or a book for a report. The information in libraries is very carefully organized. It is usually so well organized, in fact, that you can find what you are looking for even if you have only partial information, such as an author's name, a title, or just a subject. Your library may use either computers or a card catalog to organize the books. If it uses a card catalog, you look up titles in a file drawer that holds cards for all the titles and their call numbers. The call numbers are the numbers assigned them in the Dewey Decimal system; they are always printed at the top of the card.

If you know the title of the book, you simply look it up under "title entries." If you don't have a particular title in mind, you can look up material under "subject entries." Some subjects are cross-referenced, in case you can't think of the right subject name. For example, you might look up "birds" and find that the card says, "See cardinals, robins, wrens," etc. You might want to read a book by an author you like, but you can't remember the title. In that case, you'd look up your author (last name first), and find a list of all that author's books.

Many libraries are replacing their card catalogs with computers and putting their information on-line. The only difference between a card catalog and a computer is that you have to thumb through the card catalog yourself. A computer will find the same information for you at the push of a few buttons.

You don't have to be a computer whiz to find information in a library computer. You need only look under the category you want: subject, author, or title. The computer will tell you what buttons to push for the desired information. Furthermore, it can show you what the books are about and tell you if they're currently on the shelf. If your book has been checked out, the computer will tell you when it is due back.

Taking notes on what you read will help you to remember the information.

Reading

When you read something (whether a book or a magazine article or even a report), it helps if you highlight the important points. Use a marker (if you own the book or magazine) and highlight the important information. If you're reading a school textbook, take short notes on the material. Then, read over your notes and highlight *those*. Train yourself to spot the key points. Writing things down or adding color to the page helps make things stand out. You'll remember the key points better. This will be important when you have to review the material for a test or write a report yourself.

Questions to Ask Yourself

Information at school is there to help you; you can make better use of it by understanding how that information is organized. 1) Do you make good use of your school library, or do you find it confusing? 2) Are you familiar with time-saving information devices, such as computer terminals, in your library? 3) What kinds of techniques can help you to retain important information you have read?

Organizing Information in School

LEE HAD TO DO A SCHOOL REPORT ON THE REASON why a new high school should be built. He was relieved that he didn't have to give his presentation until the last day. Listening to the other students in his class give their reports, he realized that they often put their classmates to sleep. They had all organized their reports in the same way. First, they discussed how the old building was too small and in poor condition. Then they talked about how a new building would be better.

Lee agreed with the points his classmates made, but he was determined to have a more interesting presentation. Rather than starting out by talking about the old school, he thought, why not talk about the new school? He decided to write an introduction about going to the new school. He described walking into the modern building and taking an elevator up to the computer center on the school's fifth floor. It got everyone's attention. Nobody before Lee had imagined what going to a new school would actually be like. In his speech, Lee said that this was his dream about the new school. He described waking up from the dream and coming to the old school, where workers were removing peeling lead paint and his class had to meet in the hallway because there wasn't enough classroom space. Everyone laughed. It was a creative and interesting speech. Lee's teacher rewarded him with an A. And his fellow students even applauded. It made Lee realize that a little reorganization and creativity could work wonders.

Making Reports

When writing a report, you need to make your points in an organized manner. If you just list your data (even if it's accurate), it could seem boring to the listener who might not be able to follow your points.

For that reason, you need to know your key points ahead of time. The usual way to start a report is to make an outline. You list your key points, then you add supporting ideas that explain those points. When you think you've covered your topic, go back and make sure the order is logical. Some people write reports in chronological order. They start with what happened first, then go on to cover what happened next and what happened last. Some people put the most important point first, then the next most important point and so on. The good thing about an outline is that it gives your report a structure. People can see where you're going with your ideas.

Here's an example of an outline:

Natural Disasters in American History

Disasters occurring in the early 1800s

Floods

Windstorms (tornadoes and hurricanes)

Fires

Bombings/cave-ins

Disasters occurring in the mid-1800s

Floods

Windstorms

Fires

Bombings/cave-ins

Disasters occurring in the late 1800s

Floods

Windstorms

Fires

Bombings/cave-ins

(This outline uses both chronological order— starting from first to last—and subject headings. Each section covers the same types of disasters, so the reader comes to expect a complete discussion under each time frame.)

Another way of writing a report is to use an idea

wheel. An idea wheel is like an outline, but instead of listing key points in an orderly fashion, you write them down as you think of them. You start with the title in the center of the page. Then you jot down key points branching out from the title. You add defining points by writing them underneath the key idea. Once you've thought of all your points, you decide how you want to arrange them. Then you can make an outline.

An idea wheel would look like this:

"Why we need a new high school"

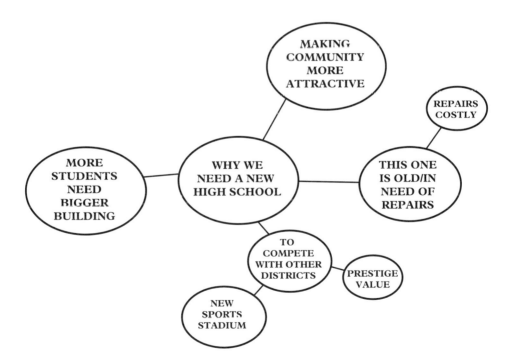

The advantage of an idea wheel is that you don't have to determine the order of your points until you have all your ideas.

When you have your points in mind for your report, you're ready to write. People tend to remember *the first and last points* that speakers make. Thus, your first point should be your most important, and your last point can be a summary.

Be direct in your writing. Use ordinary words (not words you have to look up in a dictionary). Use short sentences, especially if you're giving directions. People can get confused by sentences that go on for a whole paragraph.

Finally, think of props you can use with your speech. Most people understand things better when they have something to look at: either an object or a chart with key points outlined.

Studying for Tests

Being organized can help cut down the time you spend studying for tests. If you've already highlighted the important points, you need only review your highlighted notes.

Sometimes it helps to make a time line for your test, as it's easier to remember facts when you can see them on paper. This is especially true for history exams. Draw a line across your paper and jot down what happened first, next, and so on. If two events take place around the same time, you can see how one might have affected the other.

The more information you can organize into categories, the better you'll remember it.

A time line concerning battles in the War for Independence might look like this:

1775	1776	1777	1778	1781
Battle of Bunker Hill	Washington crosses Delaware	Valley Forge; Battle of Saratoga	Clark defeats British on frontier	Cornwallis surrenders at Yorktown

Questions to Ask Yourself

Reports and speeches are two ways students are often expected to organize information. 1) How might you make a speech interesting if you are assigned a topic that other students find boring? 2) How can an outline help you write an effective report? 3) Do you feel that your teachers and fellow students understand what you have to say, both orally and in writing?

Organizing Your Life

JAIME, MICHAL, AND JARRETT ARE SIBLINGS WHO all play soccer. During soccer season, a lot of information is generated. Each player has a separate schedule of games. Sometimes, Jaime and Jarrett take refreshments to their games. Sometimes, Michal is traveling to one city while Jaime is traveling to another. Each player has a coach, an assistant coach, and a team manager, who might need to be contacted for various reasons.

The family realized that they had so many numbers and schedules floating around that they never knew who was playing where or when. The kids' parents were tired of being informed at the last minute that they had to make thirty sandwiches by next Saturday, or that they needed to drive twenty miles to the next city the following weekend. There had to be a better way.

One Saturday, the family sat down and talked about how they could organize all the things going on during soccer season. It would be easier, they all agreed, if they could actually see what was

A wall calendar can help remind you and your family of important appointments and events.

happening. They needed a visual aid. Jaime volunteered to make a master calendar on which all of their games would be entered. But how could they tell at a glance which games required travel or snacks? Jarrett, who was considered the artist of the family, came up with the idea of making symbols. An away game was symbolized by a drawing of a little car. If refreshments were needed, a drawing of an apple was added. These visual cues helped the kids' parents to figure out what they needed to do— with plenty of time to do it.

The last thing the family did was to make a master list of all the coaches, assistant coaches, team managers, and team captains. Next to each name was the phone number and a description of what information each could provide. For example, the team managers could answer questions about equipment or travel arrangements; the coach would be called if a player was sick and had to miss a game. This master list was placed in a file marked "Soccer Teams." Using visual cues, a calendar format, and a filing system, the family was able to relax a little during what was usually a stressful time.

Ways to Organize Your Life

1. Keep a calendar near the phone so that you always know what's coming up. If you baby-sit,

An organizer or calendar may be a good investment to help you keep track of the many kinds of information in your life.

Practice developing a system of organization with something you collect, such as photographs.

you don't want to take a job when you had planned to go roller skating with your friends. Write all engagements on this one calendar. If your whole family jots down their meetings, games, and other plans, you'll have an easier time coordinating things. Calendars are also good as reminders for important birthdays and deadlines. If you need to buy a gift or remember the date of an exam, put it on the calendar.

2. Assignment books are the best way to keep track of homework. If you write yourself a note about

an assignment and stick it in your textbook, you might not remember to take the book home in the first place. If you have everything in an assignment book, you can check the book before packing up to go home each day.

3. Artists' portfolios can be used to hold your best school papers over the years. These folders are big enough to hold artwork as well, so you won't end up bending and folding things. You can store the portfolio under your bed. At the end of each year, go over the material and save only the best. As you keep adding to it, you may have to throw away some items.

4. If you buy tickets to upcoming events (concerts, games, or plays), staple the tickets to the calendar so you'll know where they are.

5. To get yourself in the habit of organizing data, try organizing your room. Start with your CDs or tapes. Organize them according to type of music, or alphabetize them (by title or musician). Just be sure to remember how you've filed things. It won't do much good if you can't recall your system.

   If you have a lot of books, group them according to subject or alphabetize according to author.

   Organize your photos, particularly if you don't keep them in an album. Write the date of the picture (at least the month and year) and the occasion on the back of each. Date every picture even if you think you couldn't possibly forget the occasion.

When you make a major purchase, staple the sales slip to the warranty and file them with the users' manual. You can either keep all your users' manuals together in a clearly labeled box or keep the manuals (and warranties and sales slips) underneath the products themselves.

6. Aside from classes, you can practice your report-writing skills when you take the minutes of club meetings. Here's where an idea wheel saves you time recording the points of the meeting. All you have to do is jot down the main ideas and then add little lines to define those ideas. After the meeting, you can tie all the points together into a report. Making idea wheels trains you to note the main ideas in a report or speech and look for the supporting points.

These are simple steps to take to organize your world so that you can hang onto all that important information. It may seem time-consuming at first to label and store all the data, but you'll save time when you have to retrieve the information.

Questions to Ask Yourself
You probably have many things you need to do

each day. Organization skills can help you to prioritize your activities and get things done on time. 1) What are your most important tasks every day? 2) Do you feel that you never have enough time— or that you sometimes have too much? 3) Do you have a collection of something (books, photos, magazines) for which a system of organization could be developed?

Organizing Your Work Environment

SANDY CARRIED A STACK OF CHARTS OVER TO THE filing cabinet. She found the F's and filed "Fennimore." She found the T's and filed "Tyler." She made her way through the pile of charts until she came to "St. Martin." She wondered, should that chart be filed with the "Saint" spelling or with the "St" spelling? She decided to put it under "St."

The following week a co-worker complained that Michael St. Martin's chart had disappeared.

"I just filed that chart last week," Sandy said.

"Well, where did you put it? It's not with the other St. Martins."

Sandy went over to the filing cabinet. "Of course, it is. It's right here." She pulled out the missing chart.

Gail frowned. "Don't you know to file 'St' under 'Saint?' I could have been looking for this all day."

Filing Systems

If you ever want to keep track of information, you'll have to develop a filing system. Sometimes manage-

A cluttered work environment can make it difficult to keep track of tasks.

ment has a filing system already in place; all you have to do is follow it. As you can see from the above example, the rules may vary. If your work-place files alphabetically, make sure you know how they file the "St. Martins". What about the "Mc" and "Mac" spellings? Which comes first? Or do they put them together under "MAC" whether the person spells his name "Mc" or "Mac"? You may not think it's a problem, but if you (or anyone else) want to find the chart again, you have to file it the way everyone else does.

Maybe you'll have the opportunity to set up a filing system yourself. Instead of the alphabetical system you might prefer to file material by *subject*. For example, you might keep files covering current accounts, inactive accounts, past due bills, sales figures, annual reports, and so on. In order for others to find information as easily as you, make sure you use a system they understand.

For example, if you want to keep track of your warranty information, will you file it under "War-ranties" or the specific brand name "Sears products"? Make sure people using your file follow the same plan; otherwise, things will be misfiled and lost forever.

Overstuffed Files

Some people hang onto every piece of information

that crosses their desk. If they can't pass it to someone else, they simply file it. In no time, the files fill up with unnecessary information.

To prevent overstuffing your files, set aside some time each month to glance through the files, throwing away information you no longer need to save. It helps to write a "discard date" on each piece of paper you file. That way you'll immediately know when it's time to throw it out. Other people trim their files each time they have to file something. Whenever they spot a note, letter, or memo that is out of date, they pull it from the file and throw it away.

Computers

Not only can you gather information on computers, you can store it in them as well. You can store the information two ways: by printing the data and filing it (more paperwork), or by saving the information on diskettes. (Then, of course, you label and file the diskettes.)

Computers were supposed to save paperwork, but if you're not careful, they can just create more. If you store information on backup diskettes (in case something happens to the first diskette), you don't have to keep a printed copy as well. Printed copies take up more space than diskettes.

Be sure to file the diskettes so that you know where the data is. You might keep a master list of all the information you've stored. It'll be easier to refer to this master list than looking at every diskette. Label each diskette with each file it contains. Keep the same types of information on each diskette. For example, keep all letters to Company A on one diskette. Keep the minutes from various meetings on another diskette and copies of reports on still another.

To preserve your office from overflowing with diskettes, be sure to delete information you no longer need. Put a "delete date" beside each file name on the diskette. That way, you'll know when to purge the material. Deleting is as simple as inserting the diskette into the computer, locating the correct file, and pushing the delete button.

Creating an Uncluttered Environment

A cluttered desk sends the message that you're not on top of things. You can lose track of important letters, memos, and charts when you let papers pile up around you. If you handle a lot of paperwork at your desk, buy some in/out baskets. As the baskets fill up, handle the work immediately. Divide the material into four convenient piles: TO FILE, TO DO, TO READ, TO PAY, for example. Set aside time each day to file so that the pile doesn't get so high that you balk at doing it. In the TO DO pile, decide what must be done and do it: Make the phone call, write the memo, or do the research. You can take the TO READ pile home with you (and ask if you can throw things away once you've read them or done what was asked). Stay on top of the TO PAY pile. Either pay bills as they become due, or pay at a set time each month. Make notations on your calendar (and attach the bills) if you don't intend to pay some for a while.

Keep forms that you use regularly in your desk drawer. If you have them organized in file folders (and the folders clearly labeled), you won't have to look through other papers to find the form you need each time.

A knowledge of filing and computers will help you organize and store important information around you. When your work environment is well organized, your performance is bound to improve. An organized work space implies an organized mind.

Questions to Ask Yourself
Workplaces must often store and organize large amounts of material. Individual employees are also responsible for organizing their own information. 1) What kinds of information organizing systems are used at your workplace? 2) Why is it important that everyone in a workplace use the same organizational system? 3) Do you find that your work environment gets easily cluttered?

An inventory helps a store to keep track of its stock.

Keeping on Top of Jobs

LARRY POWERS SPENT HIS SUMMERS MOWING lawns. His work was good, so he usually had more jobs than he could handle. Some days he mowed three sets of lawns, and people wondered how he could keep his jobs straight.

Larry's secret was the mini-organizer he carried with him. Whenever he was given a job, he marked it down (estimating how long it would take). When other people called him, he checked his book to see where he could best fit them in. He was so used to writing everything down in his mini-organizer that he even recorded his dates with girlfriends there. And he never messed up.

Keeping Track of Tasks

No matter what kind of work you do, you'll do better if you can stay on top of all the tasks. Whether you baby-sit, detail cars, or sell clothes at the department store, you'll accomplish more by setting an agenda for yourself. Larry used a mini-organizer to keep track of his jobs. You don't have to buy an expensive work organizer. A simple sheet of paper will do. Just write down the tasks you want to accomplish that day, then number the tasks according to importance. (Don't leave the hardest or most important items for last. Get them out of the way first.) Keep your list where you can readily see it. It's of no use buried under a pile of notes.

Sample agenda for department store clerk:

Check incoming orders and hang clothes.	(2)
Call other stores re: suit (size 8) for	
customer: Stone	(1)
Go over customer files and update	
information.	(6)
Make an appointment for evaluation with	
manager.	(4)
Relieve Cathy in Sportswear at 6 p.m.	(3)
Arrange for vacation in August.	(5)

This works even for baby-sitters. Keep a notebook handy to record important numbers (where to reach the parents) and notes regarding the children's care (bedtimes, baths, dinner choices). Make an agenda if the parents ask you to help out with a few chores. That way you can keep track of the tasks.

Keeping Track of Records

Even with a part-time job, you'll have plenty of records to keep track of. Use a long envelope to hold all of your paycheck stubs. (The stubs contain data regarding your social security withholding, state and federal tax deductions.) At the end of each year, keep the last stub and throw the rest away. This last stub will have all the information you need for tax purposes. Then start saving for the next year.

Patterns of Information

Yolanda got a summer job working at a café around the corner from a movie theater. Her job was to serve desserts and keep the dessert case stocked. Her first night on the job, she noticed that business was very slow at certain times and very busy at other times. Around nine-thirty, in fact, it got so busy that she ran out of desserts and had to keep customers waiting while she ran back to the storeroom to take more out of the refrigerator. Her manager came up to her afterward and asked her how things had gone.

"It was okay," said Yolanda, "except I really wasn't expecting that rush of people at nine-thirty. It was so slow before that I just assumed it wasn't a busy night."

"That's how it is here most nights," her boss

A pattern of information can be used to determine when a restaurant may be slow or busy.

said. "It's pretty slow until the movie is over. The seven o'clock show is the most popular, so when that gets out, we get a rush of people. We'll be busy again when the nine o'clock movie is over—around eleven or eleven-thirty."

Yolanda thought about this information. How could she use it to make her job easier? There must be a better way, she thought, than standing around bored and then running around like crazy. After her first week on the job, she had a system figured out. She knew that the chocolate cake was the most popular, so she made sure that she had a few extra on hand behind the counter. She knew that she sold at least ten pieces of each kind of cake during the rush, so she put those ten pieces on plates and had them ready to go. She spent the slow hours making sure that she had enough clean plates, forks, and knives, and slicing the cakes beforehand, because she knew she did an uneven job when she was rushed.

Yolanda became more efficient at her job because she was able to recognize a pattern of information. She learned that business at the café was directly affected by the showings at the movie theater. Her boss told her what the pattern was, and she was able to use this information to be better prepared on the job. Her boss even commented that before Yolanda came, people often were frustrated by the

long wait and walked out. But she was so well prepared for the rush that everyone was served with
very little wait. After her first month on the job,
Yolanda had earned herself a raise.

Questions to Ask Yourself

Being efficient, organized, and flexible will make
you stand out to your employer. 1) Which of your
tasks do you find the most difficult to accomplish?
2) What is a pattern of information you have noticed at your job? 3) Do you have an idea you could
share with your boss that would help you to serve
customers better or make you more productive?

Getting the Job

6

CHELYNN WAS APPLYING FOR A TEACHING POSITION in the local school district. She knew that half the graduates of her college wanted that job, so she decided to make her résumé stand out from the rest. Unfortunately, instead of emphasizing her strong points, she bought colored paper and a new print wheel.

Chelynn's résumé *did* stand out. Her bright red paper with silver designs around the edges certainly caught people's eye. But, because she hadn't bothered to emphasize her strong points, the search committee members simply skimmed the résumé and set it aside.

Writing a Résumé

Most people don't get a chance at a job until they've sent in their résumé. Therefore, your best shot at getting the interview is writing a strong résumé to show the employer that you're someone the company would be interested in.

Never mind the gimmicks. It's more important to organize the data. At the top of the page, give your name, address, and telephone number. Below that, cover three essential areas: Education, Work Experience, and Background Experience. This is where you emphasize your strengths.

If you have excellent educational credits (especially if you graduated with honors from a well-respected college), put that section first. However, if you've held jobs that directly relate to this position, put your Work Experience first. If your strengths are your abilities (activities, hobbies, and volunteer work), put your Background Experience first. You want to draw attention to your best points, and you do that by putting those up front in your résumé.

In the Education section, list your degree and the name of the school. Don't mention the sports you played there or the fraternity you joined unless the information pertains to the job.

In the Work Experience section, include all your jobs, starting with the present and going back to your first job. (If you've held a lot of jobs, hit the highlights. You don't want to give the interviewer the impression you're a job switcher.) Include volunteer work, especially if it pertains to the job you're applying for. Nurses should mention their work as candy stripers. Teachers should mention their years tutoring other students.

You can strengthen a résumé by drawing attention to your best qualities.

You don't have to mention why you left a job, at least in the résumé. Dates of employment are useful; salary figures are not. You can mention specific job duties if you like and as long as they're brief (and relate to the job you're seeking).

In the Background section, provide a general summary of your abilities. Consider everything that relates to this particular job, and lead off with your best points. If you're looking at a leadership position, think of all the times you've been in a leadership role (president of Student Government, captain of the football team, coach of a Little League team.)

That's all the information a good résumé needs. More than that, and the employer may decide it's too long to read.

Here's a sample résumé:

Jane Doe
1234 Highland Avenue
Anywhere, U.S.
1-800-555-1212

Background Experience:
Taught undergraduate classes in Education; 5 years' experience tutoring college students; 3 years' experience substitute teaching; volunteer tutoring in high school; taught Sunday School (7th grade) for 3 years. Served as president of Future Teachers Club, as well as secretary/Dramatics Club.

Education:
University of Oklahoma	1996	
Norman, Oklahoma	M.A./Teaching	
University of Oklahoma	1994	
Norman, Oklahoma	B.S./Secondary Education	
Abraham Lincoln High School	1990	

Work Experience:
University of Oklahoma   1994–present
   (teaching undergraduate classes in Education)
Norman Public Schools   1994–present
   (substitute teaching)
Dillard's Department Store   1990–1994
   (clerk, credit authorizer, manager)

Cover Letters

Send a cover letter along with your résumé. The cover letter should be brief and designed to catch the reader's interest. For example, you might mention how you organized a Teacher's Appreciation Day at your college or how you managed your friend's campaign for school board.

Organizing information is important in cover letters, too. First specify the position you are applying for, then explain why you are qualified. Refer to your résumé, but don't summarize it. Point out details of your education or job experience that directly relate to the job you are applying for. Don't forget to include information that may have been requested by the employer, such as salary range or computer skills. Close your letter with a statement emphasizing, again, your interest in the position and end on a confident note, such as, "I look forward to meeting with you" or "I am eager to contribute my skills to this position."

Be sure to write to a *person*, not a *job title*. Call the employer and find out the name of the person who does the interviews. Then address your letter to Mr. Frank Wells, instead of "To Whom It May Concern," or worse: "Dear Personnel Director."

Questions to Ask Yourself

Knowing how to organize information effectively

will get you noticed by prospective employers.
1) Why is a résumé so important? 2) What kind of
information is best to include in a résumé? 3) What
do you feel is your best quality that you would want
to emphasize in a résumé or cover letter?

Organizing for Performance

FRANK, A NURSE AT THE LOCAL MENTAL HEALTH center, was scheduled to give a talk to the community on depression.

"Make it a thirty-minute speech, and then we'll open the meeting to questions," his supervisor said.

Well, Frank certainly intended to prepare a speech, but friends stopped by one night to visit. Then, the next night he had to work late, and the night after that he watched his son play baseball. Before he knew it, he was standing in front of the audience to give his speech. He hadn't prepared a word.

Sure that he knew a lot about the subject, however, he jumped in. He mentioned some symptoms of depression, then talked about causes. Then he remembered some symptoms he'd left out. After a few more minutes, he ran out of things to say and couldn't recall what points he was trying to make.

Meanwhile, the audience grew restless. They couldn't follow his points and wondered who was next on the agenda.

Reports and Speeches

When you learn to organize your thoughts in reports and speeches, you're teaching yourself to think more clearly.

When you write reports for work, consider the key points. Just as you did in high school, make idea wheels (or outlines) to define those points. Then expand on them.

People complain that there's too much to read these days. If you need to prepare a report, keep that in mind. Make your report short and to the point. Set out your key ideas, and summarize briefly at the end. Use everyday words so your reader doesn't need a dictionary to get through your report. Use headings to give the reader a quick idea of what each section is about.

Keep your paragraphs short, leaving lots of white space on the page. People are turned off by solid blocks of print, and they often resist reading material that looks lengthy (and boring).

After you've jotted down your main ideas in outline form, write your report on a computer. In that way, you can see what it looks like before you've actually printed it. If it needs more white space, you can add more headings. If the key points are not in good order, you can move them around. Be sure you have a good summary at the end.

Writing and organizing skills you acquire in school will also be critical to your future career.

Memos

Maybe you'll never have to write a report, but you can't escape the occasional memo. A memo is a relatively informal, written note and is often used for communication within an office. Thankfully, memos are meant to be short and sweet.

Give the memo a title, so the receiver knows what it's about. Address the memo to someone specific, and indicate up front that you're the sender. All memos should start off the same:

To:

From:

Re (in regard to):

Be sure the person receiving the memo knows what you're asking for. Do you want approval for something? If so, clearly ask for approval, and leave lines (clearly marked) for the person to sign or initial.

If you only want to report to your supervisor about how a project is coming, consider phoning instead.

Otherwise, keep the memo brief. Make your points, and sign off. People don't always bother to read long memos; they file them to read later, and later never comes.

Presentations

If you're asked to make a presentation (like Frank

Memos are an informal form of office communication.

in the earlier example), think beyond the simple organization of the information. Yes, you want to make the key points, but you also want to keep your audience interested. Most people remember far more if they can *see the information at the same time they hear it.* For that reason, you might want to put your information onto charts using bar graphs or pictographs. If you're using statistics, you can compare figures in graphs so that your audience can easily grasp the comparisons.

Below are examples of bar graphs, line graphs, and pictographs. Depending on the nature of your data and the point you are trying to make, you will want to pick a display format that will be accurate and interesting to your audience. Practice using mental visualization to express information. Include pictures, graphs, symbols, and tables in school papers and projects.

Enrollment in Middle School 1992–1995

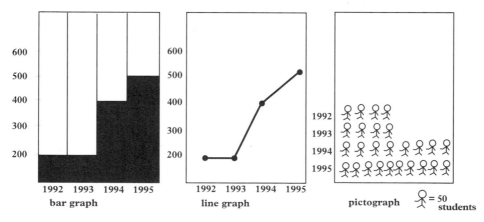

bar graph   line graph   pictograph   = 50 students

Visual aids such as slides or graphs can make an oral presentation more interesting.

Slide presentations are also entertaining if some of your information can be conveyed through photos.

In doing a presentation, think about what you want your audience to learn. If you want them to understand an event, help them to focus better with pictures of the event, maps, or charts with numbers (if numbers are an important part of the event).

It also helps to have a written agenda for your audience to refer to during the presentation. You strengthen learning by appealing to their eyes and ears at the same time. An agenda need only be an outline of your discussion. You can add some charts or diagrams to further explain the information.

Writing Letters

In business, you write letters for a purpose. Maybe you're on a fundraising drive; maybe you're trying to sell a new product; maybe you're hoping to collect on an overdue account. Whatever the purpose, make it known right at the beginning. Letters are like reports; people won't bother with them unless they think they're relevant. If you bury your key points in the middle of the letter, most people won't read that far to find them. In a paper for school, you may build up to your main argument; in a business letter, you've got to get to the point right away.

Like reports, letters need lots of white space (meaning short sentences and multiple paragraphs). Make your key points in the opening statements, and if you're asking for something (a pledge or a payment plan) be sure you specifically ask that by the letter's end. Make it easy for the reader to give you what you want. When you're not creating more paperwork for them, you'll get better results.

Keeping in Touch

Contacts are an important part of business. Whenever you meet someone you think might be important to your work, ask for her business card. Write

Business cards are useful for keeping in touch with business contacts.

the date you met her on the back of the card (and mention her association). Later, copy these cards into a file. Alphabetize your cards according to person, as well as agency. That way, if you're planning a job interview at Company A, you can look in your file to see if you know someone from Company A.

Maintain your contacts. Periodically check your files and call people to see how they're doing. Note if they've moved to a different company or have a new position. If you read in the paper that they've gotten a promotion, send a card or give them a call. This kind of keeping in touch is called "networking."

It's much easier to "network" when you keep organized.

Communication and Organization Are Connected

You already know that it is important to communicate information to co-workers in an organized way. How you choose to communicate that information is also a part of organization. Do you need a paper record of the communication for your files? Then you probably want to send a letter or a fax. If the point is simply to communicate quickly, perhaps you will want to send information over the computer, via electronic mail. If you are the recipient of electronic mail, think about whether you need a hard copy for your files before you delete the message.

Conclusion

To get ahead in today's high performance workplace, you need to manage all the information around you. Organizing that information makes it more manageable. Think *key points* whenever you tackle reports or speeches; think *files and folders* when you want to put that order into your surroundings.

Remember: the well-organized person is an asset to the high-performance workplace. These days, almost all employees have access to computers, if they don't have one at their own desk. This means that individual employees have access to a great deal of information and must maintain and organize that information. Practicing these skills now will make your transition into the high-performance workplace that much easier.

Organization and Careers

Different jobs and careers have different ways to organize information, but all jobs involve this skill in some way. An inventory is a way for a shipping clerk to organize information about stock. An itinerary is a way for a travel agent to organize information about a client's trip. A dental chart enables a dental hygienist to keep track of a patient's history.

By using different ways of organizing information in school and at work now—calendars, graphs, files, idea wheels, time lines—you'll be a pro at adapting to new systems of organization by the time you're making your way in your future career.

Questions to Ask Yourself

The high-performance workplace will give the advantage to workers who know how to organize information effectively, making good use of new information technology. 1) Do you feel comfortable using a computer? 2) What is the purpose of a memo? 3) Why is it so important to be brief and direct in workplace communication?

Glossary

bar graph Chart upon which data is recorded in bars, going from bottom to top (depending on number).

chronological order System of recording information from what happened first to what happened last.

cross reference Reference in a file to another entry containing similar information.

deletion dates Dates on diskettes indicating when the data is no longer relevant to save.

e-mail Electronic mail. Messages recorded by computer.

fax Photocopy of written information sent from one fax machine to another in a matter of minutes.

idea wheel Method of jotting down key points and then tying them together in an outline form as preparation for writing a report or memo.

line graph Chart using lines to convey information about statistics (usually plotting records, scores, or degrees).

pictograph Chart with symbols to represent statistics in a report. A key explains what each symbol represents (for example, one star = twenty points).

work organizer Notebooks with a calendar on which to record appointments and deadlines.

For Further Reading

Booher, Dianna. *Clean Up Your Act*. New York: Warner Books, 1992.

Culp, Stephanie. *Conquering the Paper Pileup*. Cincinnati: Writer's Digest Books, 1990.

Dorff, Pat; Fine, Edith; and Josephson, Judith. *File . . . Don't Pile! For People Who Write*. New York: St. Martin's Press, 1994.

Mager, N. H., and Mager, S. K., eds. *The Complete Letter Writer*. New York: Pocket Books, 1968.

Myers, Alfred Stuart. *Letters for All Occasions*. New York: HarperCollins Publishers, 1993.

Roman, Kenneth, and Raphaelson, Joel. *Writing That Works*. New York: HarperCollins Publishers, 1992.

Zinssler, William. *On Writing Well*. New York: Harper and Row Publishers, 1988.

Index

A

agenda
   for audience, 55
   for yourself, 37–38
artists' portfolios, 27
assignment book, 26

B

background experience, 44
books, organizing, 27

C

calendar, 24–26, 60
card catalog, 12, 13
CDs, organizing, 27
communication, 58–59
computer, 11, 12, 13, 33–34,
     50, 58
contacts, keeping, 56–58
cover letter, 47
cross-referencing, 13

D

Dewey Decimal System, 11, 12
diskette, 33
   delete date, 34

E

education, 44
electronic mail, 58

F

family, organizing, 22–24
fax, 58

filing systems, 30–32
   trimming, 33

G

graph, 54, 60

H

habits, formed in youth, 8
highlighting, 14

I

ideas, supporting, 17
idea wheel, 18–19, 28, 50, 60
information
   managing, 59
   organizing, 8
   patterns of, 39–42
   storing, 8
in/out baskets, 34–35

J

jobs
   competing for, 9
   getting, 43–48

K

key points, 17, 50, 56, 59

L

letters, 8, 9, 56, 58
library, 11–13

M

master calendar, 24

memos, 8, 9, 52
mini-organizer, 37, 38
minutes, club meeting, 28

N
networking, 58
notes
   highlighted, 20
   mislaying, 7
   taking, 14

O
order, chronological, 17
outline, 17, 18, 19, 50

P
photographs, organizing, 27–28
pictograph, 54
points, important, 20
presentation, 16, 52–56
   slide, 55
   props, 20

R
reading tips, 14

reports
   idea wheels with, 28
   making, 17–20
   organizing, 8
résumé, 43–48

S
salary range, 47
school, information in, 11–15
skills, information, 8–9
speech, preparing, 49
statistics, 54
symbols, calendar, 24

T
tests, studying for, 20–21
thinking, clear, 8
time line, 20–21, 60

V
volunteer work, 44

W
work experience, 44

About the Author
Carolyn Simpson teaches Psychology and Human Relations at Tulsa Junior College, Tulsa, Oklahoma. She has organized and written more than fifteen published books of nonfiction.

Photos
Katherine Hsu

Layout and Design
Kim Sonsky